# WEDNESDAY

Published by:
Ulysses Press
PO Box 3440
Berkeley, CA 94703
www.ulyssespress.com

ISBN: 978-1-64604-587-7 (trade paperback)

Printed in the United States of America
10 9 8 7 6 5 4 3

Cover Design by Noora Cox
Illustrations by Amanda Brack
Edited by Monica Sweeney

Images used under license from Shutterstock.com

# WEDNESDAY

## AN UNOFFICIAL COLORING BOOK OF THE MORBID AND GHASTLY

ILLUSTRATIONS BY
## AMANDA BRACK

ULYSSES PRESS

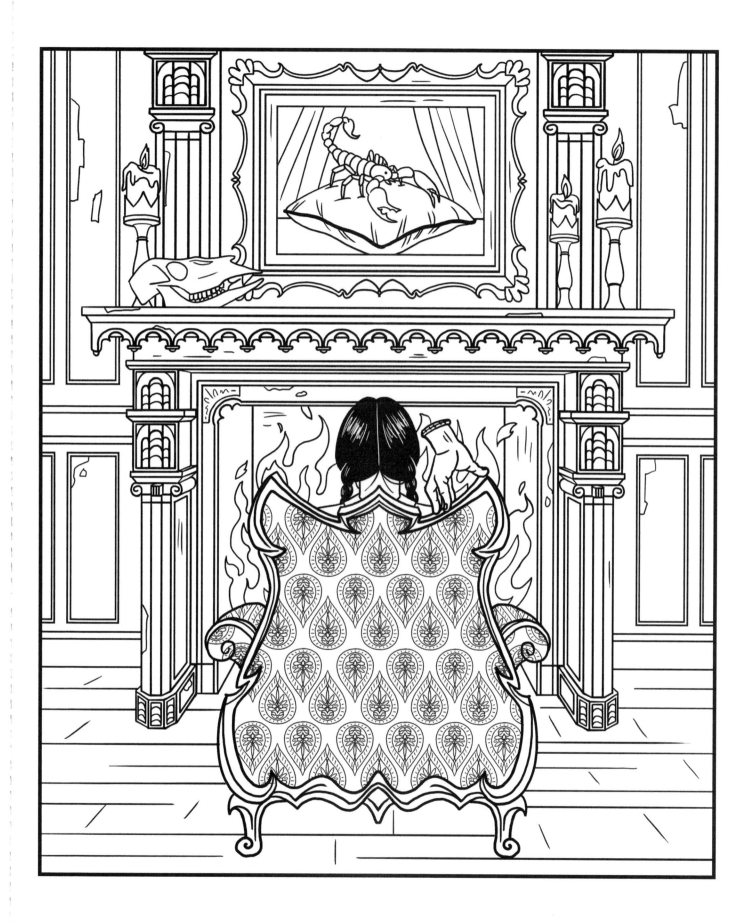